MIAMI
THE SOPHISTICATED TROPICS

Dedicated to

Danielle Chavanon

who shared this

Miami experience

from beginning

to end.

Thanks to the outstanding staff of the Greater Miami Convention and Visitors Bureau who supported this book from its inception; to Jean Berg who kept us in business in San Francisco; to our Miami friends, Marina Polvay, Christopher and Elaine Peake, Sondie Rieff, Gerry and Gwen Richman, David and Marla Bercuson, Jeffrey and Barbara Selznick, Mitchell Kaplan — without whose insight we would have lacked a balanced understanding of Miami's complexity; and to the many people who opened their doors to our cameras.

My editor, Nion McEvoy, and graphic designer, Dare Porter of Real Time Design, made all the difference in quality. Eight of Miami's finest writers gave us a many-sided view of a community that my photographs alone could not have captured.

Many thanks to Minolta who furnished my cameras, Kodak for keeping me supplied with Kodachrome, and American Airlines for transporting me to this fascinating world.

I hope you enjoy our journey to the "sophisticated tropics" as much as we did.

– Morton Beebe

MIAMI
THE SOPHISTICATED TROPICS

MORTON BEEBE

Chronicle Books • San Francisco

CONTENTS   ESSAYS

Continued . . .

Above: "The ethnic mix of Miami is one of the elements which attracted me to this book project. While at times this mix creates conflict, it also makes Miami the dynamic place it is."— *Morton Beebe.*
Below: Miami International Airport is the hub for major airlines flying to South America, the Caribbean and Europe.

AN INTRODUCTION TO MIAMI BY MORTON BEEBE

Approaching the coastline of south Florida by air from the west over the Gulf of Mexico, I was stunned by the sight of Ten Thousand Islands and the vast, lush expanse of "original" Florida. Before us the Everglades filled the horizon but for a lone, two-lane highway known as the Tamiami Trail, crossing the state from west to east.

Midway along the Trail, where the Everglades National Park meets the outskirts of Greater Miami, I could see the home of the descendants of Florida's first inhabitants. The Miccosukee Indian Reservation shares boundaries with modern Miami and the primal Everglades.

Our flight path into Miami's International Airport followed the historic Trail, seeming to pass through time from dense, primeval swamps to busy twentieth century thoroughfares. Marshes gave way to canals and streets. Land changed from bayous to farms, housing tracts, and industrial parks. As we prepared to land, the Tamiami Trail continued to the sea, through the Latin community known as Little Havana. The Trail heads beyond the Miami River, with its elegant condominiums and financial center skyscrapers, via causeway to Claughton Island, the newest man-made island on Biscayne Bay.

Seeing Miami for the first time in thirty-five years, I had to revise my image of it as a retirement community to reflect the reality of it as a "sophisticated tropics" — a meeting place of the Americas. It joins the primitive and the modern; the native and the immigrant; the financially sober and the wildly celebrant; the North, Central, and South Americas. Its warm days and nights encourage the vibrant, sensual, elegant enjoyment of life. ❖

View of South Miami Beach from South Pointe Tower. On Saturdays and Sundays, many of the area's young people gather at this end of the beach to enjoy the volleyball nets and bar of Penrod's. University students from around the nation come here during spring break.

Top left: Freedom Tower watches over Biscayne Bay, with Miami Beach in the background. The tower, built in 1925 for the *Miami Daily News*, became the processing station for Cubans entering the U.S. in the 1960s. Restored in the late 1980s, it is now one of Miami's major landmarks.

Bottom left: In May, the poinciana trees between Brickell Avenue and Interstate 95 turn bright red. The Metrorail and freeway, going toward Coconut Grove and South Miami, overlook the area.

Right: Biscayne Bay by Bill Baggs Cape Florida State Recreation Area. Every day, hundreds of speedboats and sailboats cross the emerald green bay.

Moon over Miami. Biscayne Bay reflects the lights from downtown high-rises, Bayside, and Freedom Tower.

Miami is a city of colors. *Left: Miami Line*, a neon sculpture by Rochne Krebs, brightens the Metrorail bridge in front of CenTrust Tower. Built by I. M. Pei, CenTrust Tower is lit in colors that express the events of the day. *Opposite, top*: CenTrust Tower is illuminated with patriotic colors. The *Miami Line* sculpture and the lights of northwest Miami are seen in the background. *Opposite, center*: The tower celebrates American Institute of Architects' week. *Opposite, bottom*: It recognizes an unknown function.

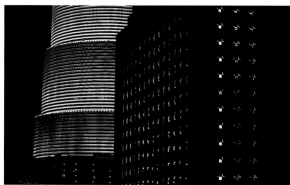

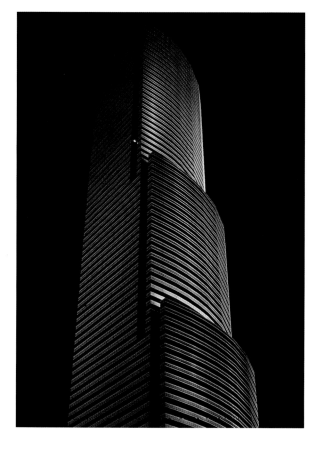

ALL THIS AND A RAINBOW, TOO BY BETH DUNLOP

In 1980, when I became the *Miami Herald's* first architecture critic, Miami was a very different place than it is today. Back then—it seems like just yesterday—downtown Miami had a gap-toothed skyline, with wide spaces between the buildings. The tallest building was 1 Biscayne Tower at thirty stories, not Southeast Financial Center soaring to fifty-five stories. The building boom on Brickell Avenue, now shimmering blocks of steel and glass towers, had barely begun.

In Miami Beach, the Art Deco District was a well-kept secret to all but a few of us. In the suburbs, everybody wondered if there would ever be much built west of the turnpike. Of course, there was the Greater Miami Opera, and there were museums of history, art, and science, an orchestra with a start-and-stop season, a little bit of local theater. It all added up to the beginnings of a strong cultural tradition, but it was just a start.

Think back. Even a partial list of what we didn't have in 1980 is pretty incredible to ponder, as bench marks of progress: Bayside, Metrozoo, Metrorail, the Miami Arena, Joe Robbie Stadium, the Knight Center, the Cultural Center, the New World Symphony, the Miami City Ballet, the Florida Philharmonic Orchestra. I could go on.

Today Miami is known as a center of architecture, of culture, as a place to watch for new designers, musicians, choreographers, dancers. Its colorful sunlit, sometimes even insouciant buildings became famous, worldwide, as the television setting of "Miami Vice." But behind that celebrated glitter, there was serious work going on, the building of a city. We have stepped forward, with enormous strides which I have always thought of as a triumph over the worst of odds.

I am not a native Miamian. I've now been here almost fifteen years, and in many ways I am still a newcomer. But my

Images of downtown. *Above*: Southeast Financial Center is the tallest high-rise. *Right, top to bottom*: Halloween celebrants; mounted police, who regularly patrol the downtown area; Spanish and English signs vying for attention; children competing in a city-sponsored sidewalk drawing contest. *Opposite*: Palm trees are everywhere.

son is a native, and he sees Miami with all the wonderment an eight-year-old can muster. He doesn't remember a Miami that didn't have Metrorail or Metrozoo; he simply enjoys music and dance without knowing of the struggles to establish an orchestra or a ballet company. For him, the New World Symphony, the Florida Philharmonic Orchestra, and the Miami City Ballet are part of life.

When my son was six, we took a family trip to Boston, one of those whirlwind city visits—six museums, the aquarium, the market, the waterfront, even a historic cemetery. We saw snow in April and bundled up as we tromped through city streets. My son was thrilled by it all. He began trying to figure out a way to move Boston south. But then, as we drove home from the Miami Airport, across the Julia Tuttle Causeway, Miami cast its uncanny spell.

"Mom," he said, "I think I like Miami better. They light the buildings at night, and besides, there's a rainbow on a bridge."

All this and a rainbow too.

Out of the mouths of babes come riveting truths. For there is so much here that is so splendid, enough that it sometimes seems we almost can't see it. ❖

Miami downtown.
Left: Children playing in a fountain at José Martí Park on the edge of Little Havana and the Miami River.
Right: The outdoor sculpture *Dropped Bowl with Scattered Slices and Peels*, by Claes Oldenburg and Coosje Van Bruggen.

Above: One of many drawbridges over the Miami River, each painted a different color. Cargo ships, tugboats, and pleasure craft share the river. *Opposite, top left:* Miami is a city of innovative architecture. CreditBank Tower on Biscayne Boulevard designed by Miami's Arquitectonica. *Opposite, top right:* The Sofitel Hotel. *Opposite, center right:* Children making sidewalk chalk drawings at a sculpture unveiling. *Opposite, bottom:* Dupont Plaza seen through the open arch of the Southeast Financial Center.

The Hyatt Regency swimming pool, overlooking the Miami River, is on a cement slab elevated above a Native American burial ground discovered during the pool's excavation.

24

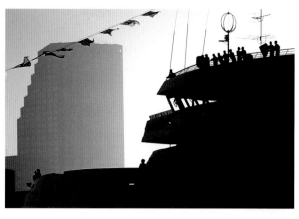

Saturday and Sunday are cruise-ship days in Miami. At dawn the ships line up along the jetties of the Port of Miami, and unload their sleepy, tanned passengers. The cabins are cleaned, the supplies are restocked, and by late afternoon a new group of jetlagged, sun-starved passengers comes on board.

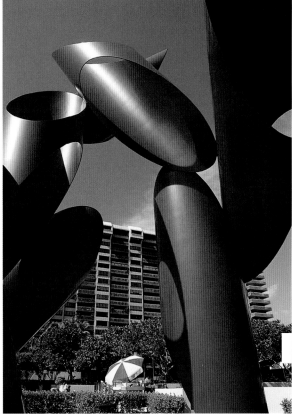

At the northeast corner of Coconut Grove is Grove Isle, a small private island with three condominium towers and a hotel. The owner, a serious art collector, has placed fifty sculptures by contemporary artists on the grounds. *Clockwise from left: Hammering Man by Jonathan Borofsky, Argosy by Alexander Liberman, Cloud by Masao Gozu, Journey's End by Ilan Averbuch, The Promise by William Tucker, and an untitled piece by Mark Di Suvero.* Both residents and visitors come to tour the collection and walk through the sculpture garden.

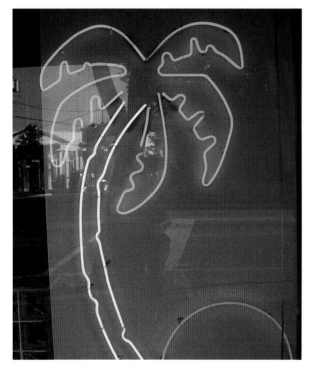

BUT WE LIKE MIAMI BY DAVE BARRY

Nearly ten years ago, my family and I decided to move to the Miami area from Glen Mills, Pennsylvania, a small town in suburban Philadelphia. When we told our friends and neighbors about this decision, they never said: "Great!" Or: "How nice for you!" What they said was: "WHY?!!!" They thought we were fools.

This is the famous South Florida Image Problem you have heard so much about. It is definitely real. I mean, these people live next to *Philadelphia,* the only city in the United States ever to protect a neighborhood from housing violators by dropping a bomb on it, yet they all recoiled at the very name *Miami,* as though we had told them we were moving to a condo in Beirut.

"But we *like* Miami," we would tell them. "We want to move there."

People tell us we live in a Nice Neighborhood. Our neigh-

South Miami Beach is a photographer's paradise. Art Deco buildings with sun-drenched pastel colors, ocean sunrises, luminous pools, and large neon signs all seem intended to act as exquisitely vivid backgrounds. The photographer need only place a model in the right spot.

bors are very insistent on this point. "You're going to like this neighborhood!" they say. "It's very nice!" They seem blind to the fact that it is located in a swamp at sea level. There is a good deal of evidence for this. Large crabs routinely saunter across the road in front of your car, and at first you think: "Hey! Isn't that funny! Crabs, here in a residential neighborhood!" Then you realize that the crabs *belong* here. They're chuckling under their breath, saying: "Look at those jerks! They bought a house *here!* At *sea level!*"

Of course we have flood insurance, but as it was explained to me at the ritual settlement ceremony when we bought our house, flood insurance does not cover you for damage caused

MEET ME IN MIAMI

To many people, Miami is the resort of retirees. But to the observant eye, it is a mix of diverse ages and races, each group celebrating its customs. In South Beach, one can encounter young people using roller blades for transportation, elderly women fending off the sun with umbrellas, students playing on the beach, older people walking in pairs along the boardwalk, and residents of all ages enjoying their neighborhood. At night, young Miamians hang out at the many cafes on Ocean Drive.

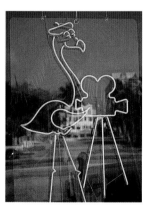

by the following:

1) Floods

2) Water coming into your house for any reason.

Here is what has me really worried: The crabs are eating our yard. I mean this sincerely. For some crab reason, they are constantly digging these tunnels, and eventually the yard will become a vast network of crab tunnels, and the house is going to fall into the canal. One night we'll be inside watching cable television, and we'll hear the sound of hundreds of crabs chortling and clacking their claws together, which is how crabs convey the concept of "TIMBERRRRRRRR!" and then we'll hear a monstrous SPLASH, followed by canal water entering our recreation room. And you just know the insurance won't cover *that,* either. You just know there's a standard Crab Clause.

So I think we're going to have to hire a professional Crab Man. We already have a Bug Man, of course. You have to. Insect control down here is no job for amateurs. If I were to hit one of these fully mature subtropical cockroaches smack on the forehead with a ball-peen hammer, all I'd do is anger it. It might decide to charge, and my only chance then would be to lure it outside, in the hope that the lawn would get it.

Our lawn grows like a venereal disease. The Lawn Man comes around regularly and subdues it, after which there is a period of about two hours when you can walk safely on it, but you damn well better make sure you are standing on the driveway when it regains consciousness and starts lashing out with violent new growth tendrils.

Yes, we have a pool. It is the only furnished part of our house, featuring three attractive kickboards from Toys 'Я' Us, and we have gotten much enjoyment from it except for the one time there was a snake in there. But here's the thing about pools: When they belong to other people, you tend to think of

them as just being large fun containers of water, whereas when they belong to you, you find out that they actually contain delicate chemical balances that even the leading scientific minds of the day don't really understand. And if these balances get upset, you have to have the Pool Man come and add large amounts of chemicals that look like cocaine but cost more.

Another thing we never had in Pennsylvania is cable television. I had no idea what we were missing. They have channels on cable that will flat out show *anything*. I think the best cable shows are the ones that originate locally, the ones that have names like "Plant Beat."

There was one show, on the official Coral Gables channel, that consisted entirely of law-enforcement personnel telling you all the reasons why you should mow your lawn. This is the truth. He said that if you let your grass get too long, criminals could hide in there. Which may be true, but I bet they'd never get out. You'd come home, and a criminal would stick his head

South Miami Beach is a paradise for Art Deco aficionados. Many years of effort led by, among others, Barbara Bear Capitman, helped save these gems built during the 1930s and 1940s from destruction. To revive the area, Leonard Horowitz and other designers and architects started painting the Art Deco buildings with pastel colors and in the process developed the Miami Art Deco style. *Bottom left*: Amid the Art Deco buildings are other examples of period architecture such as the Memphis-style Coronet apartment building. *Center left*: Photographers, crews, and models can often be found surrounded by the daily bustle.

up out of your lawn and say: "Please! Help me! I'm trapped in the . . ." His voice would be cut off suddenly by a massive muscular tendril wrapped around his throat.

I guess this is starting to sound kind of whiny. I don't mean it to be. I don't want to sound like those people who voluntarily move down here to get away from cold weather, then spend all their time bitching about how hot it is. Although now that I mention it, it is pretty darned hot, isn't it? Also humid. To prevent spoilage, we've taken to keeping everything—bread, salt, aspirin, socks—

34

Most Art Deco hotels and apartment buildings between Sixth and Twenty-third streets have been preserved, even though a few were lost to parking garages and modern structures, or were abandoned.

in the refrigerator. But I'm not complaining. As I said, we really do like it here, and we hope to make lots of new friends who will come over and stand around our living room. And maybe later, if there's a cool breeze and the mosquitoes are feeling lenient, we can go outside and enjoy the sweet scents and sounds of the subtropical night. Maybe toss some meat to the lawn. ❖

Murals, trompe l'oeil images, and graffiti give liveliness and artistry to the walls of the South Miami Beach neighborhood.

Art Deco homes for the elderly, once a very common sight in South Beach, have been remodeled and converted into hotels for tourists. As a result, the rows of deck chairs facing the street are slowly disappearing. *Opposite, top left*: Facade of the Miami Beach Convention Center. *Opposite, bottom left*: Every American over forty who watched television as a child should remember Jackie Gleason's show and his famous "And a-wa-a-a-y we go!" pose which is immortalized in this figure in front of the Jackie Gleason Theater of the Performing Arts. As part of the Concert Association of Greater Miami, the theater presents world-class entertainment, including Leontyne Price, Pavarotti, Midori, the Moscow Philharmonic, and the American Ballet Theater. *Opposite, right*: The Holocaust Memorial Monument, a major addition to Miami Beach.

Miami is a "water town." West of Miami Beach, Biscayne Bay washes the coast from north to south. *Left:* Many islands are connected to the mainland by causeways. Among them are Hibiscus and Palm islands. *Opposite, top left:* Boats are anchored to the river walls of residences on the numerous inland waterways off the Miami River. On weekends the owners sail or motor up and down the waterways, sometimes stopping for lunch, cocktails, or dancing at Sundays on the bay at Haulover *(opposite, bottom)*. Fishermen anchor next to this popular spot, selling their day's catch.

Opposite, top left; and right, top and bottom: Newport Fishing Pier on Sunny Isle Beach is popular with vacationers staying in the area's moderately priced hotels. *Opposite, top right:* From Central and South America, Latins have brought a panoply of bright, joyous colors, as witnessed by this T-shirt stand on Sunny Isle Beach. *Opposite, bottom:* Penrod's in South Miami Beach often holds a wet T-shirt contest. Here winners are being announced.

From South Pointe to Surfside, with the exception of the Art Deco District, life is focused on the fluorescent, warm water of the Atlantic.

46

Right: Golden Beach, north of Miami Beach, is an exclusive residential area with a two-story height limit. It lies between the Atlantic Ocean and the Intracoastal Waterway, which links Miami to South Florida. *Opposite, top and bottom right*: Fisher Island, once owned by Carl Fisher, the developer of Miami Beach, offers elegant, secluded residences for wealthy Miamians and fashionable second homes for well-to-do visitors. The island can be reached only by car ferry. Once home, the residents park their automobiles and walk, bike, or use golf carts to get around the island. The atmosphere is one of casual elegance. *Opposite, bottom left*: Young women in a South Miami Beach swimming pool.

Contrary to its appearance, Bayside, a mall built by Biscayne Bay at the marina, draws locals as well as visitors. It also attracts many street artists, such as clowns, magicians, and singers. The mall has a small outdoor stage where local musicians perform in the late afternoon.

The King Mango Strut, probably the zaniest parade in the area, was started in 1982 by a local lawyer, Glenn Terry, as a spoof on the King Orange Jamboree Parade. It takes place every December in Coconut Grove.

Held each spring, the Dade County Youth Fair and Exposition, which began almost forty years ago as a small agricultural fair, has become an educational exposition offering family-oriented amusement.

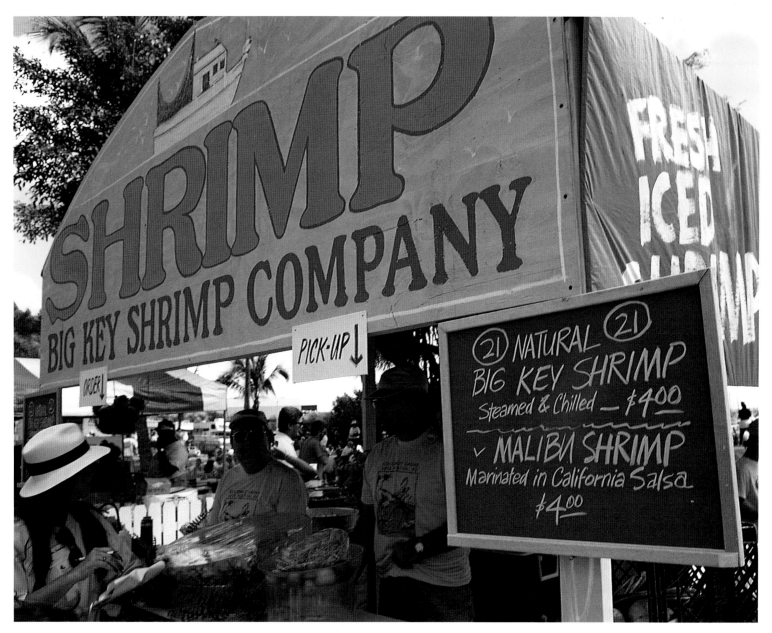

Food, fun, and sun. The Coconut Grove Art Festival, considered to be the largest art festival in the nation, takes art and food very seriously. The art on display draws a national audience. The food, referred to by the organizers as "culinary art," includes local delicacies such as conch fritters and chowder, Tex-Mex fajitas, Australian BBQ, and many other flavorful foods and drinks. Early the first morning, a group of judges walks from stand to stand, sampling every speciality. Ribbons are awarded to those judged to be offering the finest cuisine.

Sunset seen from Little Palm Island, one of many islands that make up the Florida Keys extending south into the Caribbean.

HISTORY OF THE KEYS BY GEORGE MURPHY

"Key West is intensely unlike any other place in the Union."
—Mrs. L. D. Whitson, *Away Down South,* 1886

Thousands of years ago, the seas receded, exposing the coral and limestone reef tracts which would become the Florida Keys. Although the modern recorded history of the Keys begins with Juan Ponce de León's 1513 discovery of the islands he named Los Mártires—The Martyrs—after the twisted, tortured appearance of the dense and tangled native mangrove trees, the Indian pottery and artifacts that have been excavated date back to 1200 B.C.

The effects of numerous tribes have been found, but it was largely the Calusa tribe that inhabited the Keys until the 1760s, when invading mainland tribes drove them southward, island by island, until they were massacred on the island later to be known as Key West.

Although the Florida Keys are commonly perceived as an exotic island outgrowth of Miami, it is, ironically, Miami which grew from the Keys.

Five years before the U.S. Navy first ventured, in 1835, into the wilderness at the mouth of the Miami River to establish its West Indies stockade—Fort Dallas—the city of Key West had already been chartered and surveyed. For a period of fifty years before the settlement at Miami expanded beyond several shacks and tents, Key West had become more populous than all the rest of Florida combined.

In fact, Miami's most noted pioneer, Mrs. Julia Tuttle, credited with having brought the Flagler railroad to Miami, arrived by sailboat to Biscayne Bay in November of 1891—from Key West.

With its deep-water port at the juncture of two oceans and its subtropical climate, Key West had long been a haven for pi-

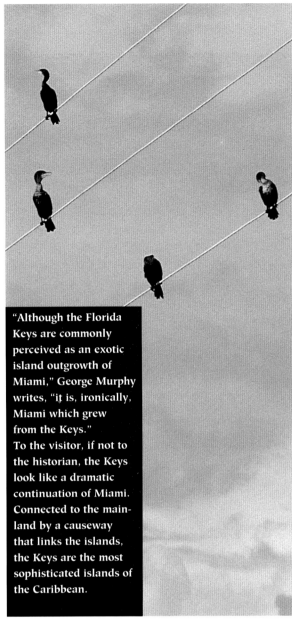

"Although the Florida Keys are commonly perceived as an exotic island outgrowth of Miami," George Murphy writes, "it is, ironically, Miami which grew from the Keys."
To the visitor, if not to the historian, the Keys look like a dramatic continuation of Miami. Connected to the mainland by a causeway that links the islands, the Keys are the most sophisticated islands of the Caribbean.

rates and for Spanish adventurers who, having found the island littered with the bleaching bones of massacred Calusa Indians, named it Cayo Hueso—Island of Bones—a name later corrupted into Key West.

Within months after the first settlement was established in 1822, the U.S. Navy sent the tyrannical Commodore David Porter, a veteran of the Barbary Coast Wars, to Key West. Porter launched a bloody and successful campaign to rid the Caribbean of piracy. Soon after, the previously risky business of shipping through the Florida Straits thrived. So, too, did the practice of "wrecking," the salvaging of valuable cargo from the innumerable ships that ventured too close to the unmarked shallows and reefs off the coast of the Keys.

In 1825, Congress enacted legislation requiring that all salvaged goods taken from wrecks be brought to a U.S. port for arbitration. For the entire Caribbean basin, that port was Key West. Soon after, as auction houses were built on the waterfront to sell the salvaged spoils from some of the richest cargos ever lost at sea, Key West became the wealthiest city per capita in America.

New England and Bahamian seamen, fortune seekers, buyers, adjusters, shipwrecked merchant sailors, and Cubans were the foundation of the ever-expanding ethnic and cultural mix of this increasingly cosmopolitan island city.

By 1831, industry had arrived: ship fitting, turtling, salt manufacturing, and cigar making. One cigar factory alone employed fifty people. Late in the next decade, it was discovered that the high-quality sea sponges used so commonly among the local population could fetch a substantial price in the North. Another industry was begun, and Bahamian "spongers" arrived in droves. By 1850, a hospital, a school, and several churches had been built and a quarter of the island had been cleared for settlement.

Dr. David Nathanson, a clinical psychologist, treats mentally disabled children at the Dolphin Research Center in Grassy Key. The children call him Dr. David. Using play with the dolphins as reward, he works with his patients to increase their attention spans, and therefore their learning abilities. Some of the children have never spoken before. Saying one word brings the joy of swimming with a dolphin.

In 1845, the war department began construction of two forts, Jefferson and Taylor, which would later serve as headquarters for the very successful naval blockade of the Confederacy. During the Civil War, as many as 299 ships were anchored at one time in the harbor at Key West, the only Union-held city south of the Mason-Dixon line.

After the war, the newly constructed navigational lighthouses led to the decline of the wrecking industry, but the Cuban cigar-making industry grew phenomenally. The subsequent immigration of thousands of Cubans during the Ten Years War in Cuba made Key West the cigar capital of the world and a haven for Cuban revolutionaries. The Cuban influence on Key West, which is bilingual to this day, can never be underestimated; in fact, it was the Cuban San Carlos Institute, established in 1871, which made Key West a culturally vital city.

By 1874, the upper Keys had been surveyed and plotted for homesteading by the government and were inhabited by Cockney fishermen and farmers who planted pineapple, melons, citrus, and coconut where they could in the otherwise petrified ground.

Fifty acres of downtown property were destroyed by fire in 1886, but by the following year, steamship service was established between Tampa, Key West, and Havana, and reconstruction of the city was vigorously underway. By 1889, there was an electric lighting plant; by 1890, a turtle-canning factory and icehouse.

All the while Miami was still a wilderness village and Indian trading post. As the city of Miami was being established, the city of Key West was again undergoing drastic change. At the turn of the century, José Martí's Cuban Revolutionary Party was running men and guns to Cuba. Then, with the explosion of the USS *Maine* in Havana harbor in 1898, the island became the pivotal military installation of the Spanish-American War.

View from Palm Isle in the Florida Keys. "Come weal, come woe; come progress, come decay; . . . nothing can mar the sky, the water, the sunrise and sunset." — *Jefferson Brown, Historian.*

It can probably be said that the Flagler Railroad gave birth to Miami. It was also the staggering and unflagging vision of Henry Flagler which finally connected the island to the continent. In 1905, Flagler began work on one of the most monumental construction feats in American history, extending his renowned railroad over a hundred miles of water and islands to a terminal located on 134 new acres of land added to the island by his dredging teams.

When the project was completed in 1912, Key West became the "Gateway to Cuba." Steamers, ferries, and cargo ships filled the harbor.

One can easily imagine the island of Key West in those days as being caught up in a dream of future success and luxury. However, a disastrous succession of events were soon to destroy Key West's thriving economy.

First, labor problems and destructive hurricanes led to the migration of the cigar industry to the Tampa area. Then, an underwater blight infected and destroyed the sponge beds, and the island's second industry died. The Florida land boom collapsed in the mid-1920s, and those few tourists who did arrive were, more often than not, just passing through to Cuba. Then came the Great Depression, with fewer and fewer trains arriving in town. By 1934, eighty percent of the population was on relief and there was even talk of abandoning the island and resettling its population. Key West, once the wealthiest city per capita in America, had come full circle. It was now the poorest.

Into this scenario stepped the handsome, eccentric, and inventive Julius Stone, director of the Florida Federal Emergency Relief Authority (FERA) and, some say, the conceptual architect of the Key West we know today. A master of publicity, Stone responded to the economic decay by issuing a federal "Surrender of Key West," which made national headlines. He dressed in Bermuda shorts (unheard of at the time and referred

For gourmets, winter in Miami and the Keys means stone crab season. Fishermen set marked traps in sheltered areas. Every day they pull up the traps, grab the crabs, remove one claw, and return the crustaceans back to the water. The crabs grow new claws that can be harvested.

to by the locals as "underwear") and organized a citywide cleaning and planting of coconut palms—then traveled the country proclaiming Key West as America's new tropical island paradise. His efforts paid off with forty thousand tourists visiting Key West in 1934.

Yet, just as the economic recovery seemed likely, nature altered the city's course once again. On Labor Day of 1935, the strongest hurricane in history hit the Florida Keys. Sustained winds of over two hundred miles an hour and "tidal waves" from the storm surge killed hundreds and tumbled the railroad into the ocean.

In 1938, the Overseas Highway opened with its world-famous Seven-Mile Bridge reconverted from railway to roadway, and Stone's vision materialized as tourists began to flock to the island.

It was during the 1930s as well that the seeds of Key West's reputation as a haven for writers and artists were sown. Renowned writers Robert Frost, Wallace Stevens, and John Dos Passos, among others, were regular visitors; Ernest Hemingway and, later, Tennessee Williams made the island their home.

After World War II, during which the military expanded control from fifty to almost three thousand acres in the lower Keys and made Key West a major convoy center, the island settled, in the 1950s, into a period of reconstruction and readjustment, focusing again on tourism—no doubt aided by President Harry S Truman's choice of Key West for his "Little White House" retreat.

In the 1960s and 1970s, smuggling was a major industry in the Keys, and the fortunes of many of the city's most successful businessmen were made as bales of marijuana were openly unloaded on the city docks. In 1980, after the Mariel Boatlift, the U.S. border patrol, searching for illegal aliens and smuggled drugs, set up a roadblock on Highway 1, which backed up

Above, left and below: The Key West Light-house. *Above, right*: One of the many pelicans that make the lighthouse area home. *Opposite, top and bottom*: Key West beach and pier. *Opposite, center*: Schooner and catamaran leaving Key West harbor for an evening sunset cruise.

traffic to and from the Keys for hours. In an echo of Julius Stone's publicity drive of the 1930s, the city fathers, reacting to the imminent financial disaster of a tourist economy, seceded from the Union, established the Conch Republic, fired one shot, ceremoniously surrendered, and applied for foreign aid. The stunt succeeded in reopening the highway, and the celebration of the event is, to this day, a city tradition.

Renowned for its frost-free pollen-less climate, azure waters, tropical flora and fauna, and sportfishing, and for its easy pace and laissez-faire tolerance of alternative life-styles, the island continued to draw a new and eclectic mix of dropouts and developers, runaways and roustabouts of all persuasions. It also attracted a new generation of artists and writers who popularized the mythology of the island. Jimmy Buffet's lament of being "Wasted away again in Margaritaville" has become a landmark goal of many visitors. There's no uptown or downtown in the Keys, no dress codes even for the finest of restaurants; acceptance is the rule and differences are to be celebrated. During October's Fantasy Fest each year, the city is as alive as New Orleans during Mardi Gras.

The island can still boast of the most unusual and eclectic population of any American city. Literally and figuratively, the Florida Keys are both the end of the American road and the tip of the American funnel. People in the Keys live not just at the edge of America but also on the edge of danger, where the next hurricane could, in the words of novelist Thomas Sanchez, "wipe the slate clean."

Daily life in the Keys still includes the nightly celebration of the sunset, where artisans, musicians, and street performers, along with visitors, pack the city pier as the famed and often glorious Key West sunsets shimmer over the Gulf of Mexico.

Over seventy years ago, historian Jefferson Browne wrote of the sun in the Keys: "When the day is done, he sinks back into

the western deep, attended by a pageantry of color that can be produced only by the Master Artist; streaks of red across cerulean blue, fade to delicate pinks and greens and soft tones of gray, whilst the sun from his place below the horizon sends his rays through the clouds, till they resemble mountains of molten gold.

"Come weal, come woe; come progress, come decay; come nature with her beauty, come man with his mistakes; nothing can mar the sky, the water, the sunrise and sunset, which make the unchanging and unchangeable Key West!" ❖

Above and below: An ocean wader's view of a Florida Keys island and pier. The local birds, in this case snowy egrets, noisily compete for the anglers' daily catch. *Right:* Typical Key West flora—hibiscus blossoms.

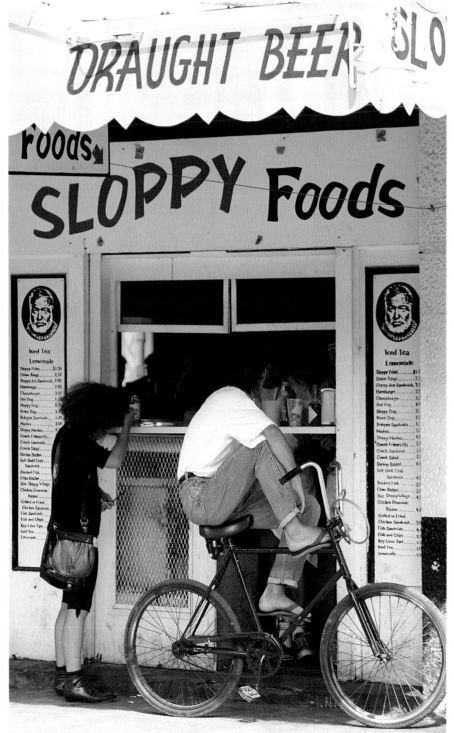

Key West street scenes: shorts, scooters, bicycles, and steel drums — all the necessities for a vacationer's tropical island sojourn.

According to Key West jargon, a conch is a person born in Key West, a Key Wester is an immigrant to the island, and everyone else is a stranger.

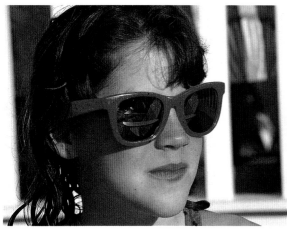

Sunset is a nightly ritual in Key West, where everyone assembles at Mallory Square Pier. Street artists entertain the crowd, and vendors display their goods for the duration of the event.

Key West has been the adopted home of numerous famous people. *Opposite*: Ernest Hemingway's residence. *Right*: John James Audubon's house. *Bottom left*: The former Little White House established by President Truman, a frequent visitor to Key West. Today, Truman Annex is the site of elegant private residences. Other famous visitors were writers Robert Frost, Wallace Stevens, John Dos Passos, and Tennessee Williams. *Bottom right*: A guard at the Truman Annex.

Top: Seminole Indians traveled to Miami in the eighteenth century. They came down the Miami River in dugouts to sell alligator skins, pelts, and bird feathers. *Left:* The family of a man named Jimmy, on the Coconut Grove waterfront. *Opposite, top:* An unidentified group of Seminoles, possibly scouts for the U.S. Army. *Opposite, bottom:* Dr. Tiger, a Seminole. — *From the Ralph Munroe Collection, Historical Association of Southern Florida.*

THE EARLY HISTORY OF MIAMI BY HOWARD KLEINBERG

So few know when it all began. Those who came in 1896 to found a city along the banks of the Miami River believe it began with them. The men who as soldiers, sailors, and airmen during World War II experienced Miami and went home at war's end to gather their families and move here believe they discovered the place. And those hundreds of thousands of Cubans who began arriving here in 1959, initially in flimsy boats and rafts, cannot imagine a Miami before the influx of exiles.

Miami always has been a place of discovery and rediscovery. For each new Miami, there had to be an old Miami to replace.

Miami's recorded history actually began—surprise!—in May 1513. That's when the Spanish adventurer Juan Ponce de León sailed into Biscayne Bay on his return south from a landfall in northern Florida, the first recorded by a European on the American continent. By comparison, no one sailed into New York City's waters until nearly a hundred years later.

When Ponce de León arrived in what would be Miami, there already were people here. They were the Tequesta Indians, and their residence in the area carbon-dates back at least ten thousand years. That Ponce de León marked this place on his map as Chequescha—his interpretation of Tequesta—documents not only his arrival but the presence of his hosts. Ponce de León may not even have been Miami's first tourist. The James Ford Bell collection at the University of Minnesota contains the controversial, anonymously drawn "Nautical Chart of 1424"—sixty-eight years before Columbus's landing—which shows landmasses closely resembling south Florida and Cuba.

Perhaps Ponce de León wasn't here first but he left the best trail. Not only was he here in May 1513, but according to the

Top left: An 1894 view of the Miami, or "Mayaimi," River from Gilbert's Wharf. *Opposite, top:* Planter's home on Elliott Key built with siding salvaged from ship-wrecks. *Below:* Rocky Bluff, Miami shoreline. — *From the Ralph Munroe Collection, Historical Association of Southern Florida.*

sixteenth century official historian appointed by the Spanish king Phillip II, Ponce de León returned at the beginning of July. That's when he logged the area as Chequescha, the name of the native cacique.

That Ponce de León was mortally wounded by Calusa Indians on Florida's west coast probably was among the reasons the Spaniards stayed away for a few decades. But when Pedro Menéndez de Avilés, while conquering Florida for Spain, arrived on its west coast in 1566, he was greeted by a white man who said he had been held captive by the Indians since 1549. Hernando Escalante d'Fontaneda, shipwrecked at the age of thirteen along with other Europeans, survived the ordeal because he learned to speak the language of the Indians. The other Europeans perished, either of natural causes or at the hands of their captors.

It was Escalante d'Fontaneda who was the first European to travel throughout southern Florida and to write about it. In 1575, he published a memoir, part of which described what was to be Miami: "Toward the north, the Mártires [Florida Keys] end near a place of the Indians called Tequesta [Miami], situated on the bank of a river which extends into the country the distance of fifteen leagues, and issues from another lake of fresh water, which is said by some Indians who have traversed it more than I, to be an arm of the Lake of Mayaimi [Lake Okeechobee]."

Menéndez's nephew, Pedro Menéndez Marqués, was dispatched to Tequesta to capture some Spanish mutineers who had settled into coexistence with the Indians. Upon arriving in October of 1566, Menéndez Marqués was greeted warmly. Three months later, he landed with Jesuit Brother Francisco Villareal and thirty soldiers to establish Christianity's first outpost on the southeast Florida coast.

The mission was built on the Miami River where the Hyatt

Bahamians settled in Miami in the late 1800s. They first lived in the shotgun houses of segregated Overtown and Coconut Grove. Bungalows later replaced the narrow shotgun houses. *Top:* Group portrait in front of Munroe's Coconut Grove boathouse. *Opposite, top two:* Sunday service at Christ Episcopal Church in Coconut Grove. *Above and opposite, bottom two:* Bahamian traditions are still in evidence today. Funerals include a musical procession to the cemetery to celebrate the deceased. — *Group portrait from the Ralph Munroe Collection, Historical Association of Southern Florida.*

Regency Hotel now stands in the downtown district. A large cross and twenty-eight houses were erected within a stockade.

Brother Villareal's mandate was to Christianize the Tequestas. A good number of the Indians were taken to Havana to be converted. But Miamians by any name are a rambunctious lot. While Menéndez de Avilés took three Tequestas to a lavish audience with the king and queen of Spain, the folks back home were not happy. The mutineers who chose to stay at Tequesta were reprieved. But for the Spanish soldiers, boredom and cultural shock set in, and soon they were feuding with the Tequestas.

In a lengthy letter to his superior, Brother Villareal began giving notice that things weren't going well. He wrote that the Tequesta children were having a difficult time learning their Catholic doctrine, that there were conflicts between Christianity and tribal practice in the treatment of the sick and dying, and that the mosquitoes were unbearable: "I passed some nights and days without being able to sleep for an hour." Arguments between the soldiers and the natives turned into conflict and soon there were killings. The Tequestas became inhospitable and the Spanish were forced to leave rather hastily.

There was one more short attempt at a mission at Tequesta a year later, but other than that, the last Spanish soldier leaving the future Miami took the flag with him. Although the Tequestas kept contact with the Spanish in Havana, Europeans were not to return to the area for a long time.

Diseases contracted through contact with the Europeans began to decimate the Tequestas until they became few in number. As the eighteenth century took hold, bands of Creek Indians, known as Seminoles, started arriving from northern Florida and brutalizing the remaining Tequestas. Fearing the Seminoles more than the Spanish, the Tequestas requested a boatlift to Havana. How ironical that seems in the face of the

boatlift that went the other way in the twentieth century. Those Tequestas who went to Cuba faced more disease and unfriendly conditions. Some returned to the Miami River; some stayed in Cuba.

Those few who returned witnessed another attempt by the Spanish to establish a mission on the river. Two priests and a company of soldiers arrived in 1743, renamed the place Pueblo de Santa Maria de Loreto, and set up a mission. It was doomed from the start. The few Tequestas who lived here were antagonistic. The Spanish decided that the mission was not worth the trouble and again left the area.

In 1763, Spain ceded Florida to England in the Treaty of Paris. England sent surveyors to their new territory, but little else. Spanish names were changed to British names. The Río Rattones, which is what the Spanish called the Miami River, became the Garbrand River.

Shortly after British rule began, the American Revolution broke out. By and large, the Miami area was unaffected. In 1784, England traded Florida back to Spain for the Bahamas. Both Americans from the north and Bahamians filtered into Florida, much to the consternation of the Spanish. They took land and ignored Spanish rule. By 1819, the Spanish had given up on Florida. They ceded it to the United States, which took Florida as a territory in 1821 and as a state in 1845.

The land north and south of the Miami River began changing hands through the honoring and selling of land grants. The land where the Spanish mission once stood near the Miami River became a plantation, and later a military outpost from where American troops struck against the Seminoles of the Everglades. Fort Dallas, named after a naval officer, had several lives through three wars with the Seminoles. As a result of the hostile action, most white settlers fled the area. In 1860, only sixty people were reported living there.

Opposite, top: The first winter visitors to Biscayne Bay, at Kirk Munroe's, 1886. *Above:* In the 1920s, Miami became the winter destination of beach lovers. Seasonal events were increased to encourage visitors to stay past winter. *Left:* Ocean Drive, looking north toward the Deauville Casino, April 1926. — *Photographs at opposite, top, and above from the Ralph Munroe Collection, Historical Association of Southern Florida. Photograph at left from the Romer Collection, Miami-Dade Public Library.*

Cape Florida Lighthouse has been watching over the southern tip of Key Biscayne since December 1825. Although sixty-five feet high, it did little to prevent shipwrecks. It was the site of the Seminole Indian attack of 1936 and is now part of the Bill Baggs Cape Florida State Recreation Area. A frequent visitor to Key Biscayne was a German officer who, during World War II, was on a submarine stationed offshore. From his periscope, he watched people playing on the beach and decided to settle there if he survived the war. He lived to fulfill his dream. — *Photograph at right from the Historical Association of Southern Florida.*

The Civil War brought limited involvement. Confederate sympathizers controlled the Cape Florida lighthouse while a Federal blockade kept the area bottled up. At war's end, the Confederate Secretary of the Treasury, John Breckenridge, made a dramatic escape from Union forces in a zigzag dash across Biscayne Bay to Cuba. What remained of Fort Dallas became a land company and trading post on the north side of the river. A pioneer named William Brickell set up shop on the south side.

It was not until the last decade of the nineteenth century that the future Miami began to take form. Widow Julia Tuttle, who purchased the land on the north shore, including the old Fort Dallas, was determined to build a city from the near jungle in which she lived. At that point, Miami's ancient, often untold history becomes linked with its contemporary history. In 1895, Tuttle convinced Henry Flagler to build his railroad to the settlement on the Miami River. The first train arrived in April of 1896, a month after construction began on Flagler's hotel, the Royal Palm.

The new frontier lured hundreds, then thousands, from upstate Florida, Georgia, and Ohio, from the Bahamas, and even from eastern Europe. A new land was opening up.

In the less than a hundred years of Miami's existence as a city, it has changed images many times—from the sleepy, quasi-southern city of the turn of the century, to a mid-twentieth century cosmopolitan playground for New Yorkers and other Northerners, to the Latin American-oriented center it is today. These parts of Miami's history are well known and often written about.

But it was hundreds of years earlier that the seeds were planted for what we have today, sown like coconuts washed ashore, by shipwrecked Spanish sailors, visionary mapmakers, Christian missionaries, and Tequesta Indians. ❖

Top: Schooners at Miami Wharf, 1926. *Left:* American Legion Parade, 1934. *Opposite, top:* During the real-estate boom of 1923, construction equipment, including Rose, the elephant, gathered for the building of the Nautilus Hotel in Miami Beach. *Opposite, bottom:* Coral Gables developer George Merrick's first sales were at auctions. "Doc" Dammers was the auctioneer. — *From the Romer Collection, Miami-Dade Public Library.*

A new Miami has risen on the northwest corner of the Miami River estuary. From left to right, the Hotel Inter-Continental, Miami Center, and Southeast Financial Center occupy the point of the peninsula. Across the mouth of the river, Brickell Avenue is lined with architecture from the past and present. The Sheraton Brickell Point and Barnett Bank Tower frame the First Presbyterian Church and Preschool. In the foreground is Claughton Island, a newly developed residential and office building island.

MIAMI, THE MAGIC CITY BY ARVA MOORE PARKS

Miami was little more than a scraggly excuse for a village when it picked up its first and most enduring nickname: "The Magic City." It must have seemed like magic, though, the way things were happening so fast. In October 1895, Julia Tuttle, who owned a large tract of land on the north bank of the Miami River, finally struck a deal between herself, William Brickell, who owned the land on the south bank, and industrialist Henry Flagler. In exchange for land, Flagler agreed to bring his railroad to Miami, build a luxury hotel, and lay out a new town.

In April, a month after Flagler's men arrived to break ground for the Royal Palm Hotel, the train reached Miami. Every day, scores of eager newcomers stepped off the train and into the promise of paradise at the end of the road. Businessmen fought over a chance to open in Tuttle's hastily constructed, wild-west style, wooden storefronts that were jammed shoulder to shoulder along the town's first cleared street (now Miami Avenue). Before July ended, 424 men, almost half of them black, had signed up to prove that Miami had enough voters to incorporate as a city. Three hundred and sixty-eight showed up at a July 28 meeting to make it official and "The Magic City" was born.

Flagler's 700-foot-long, five-story, wooden Royal Palm Hotel rose skyward, completely dwarfing everything else in sight. By December, the hotel was almost finished—its bright yellow siding, green shutters, and red mansard roof absolutely glowing (along with predictions of Miami's future) in the bright winter sunlight. Unfortunately, the euphoria was short-lived.

On Christmas Eve, fire broke out in Brady's grocery store and spread instantly to the Bank of Bay Biscayne next door. The townspeople, along with Julia Tuttle herself, battled the flames until the last spark died out. When the smoke cleared, it was

Aventura is the northernmost community of Dade County/ Greater Miami. Its prestigious high-rise condominiums are built on the perimeter of the golf course of the exclusive Turnberry Isle Resort and Club. Some of the world's largest yachts anchor at Turnberry Marina.

apparent that most of the brand-new town had burned to the ground.

Despite the setback, the Royal Palm Hotel opened on January 17. The twinkling electric lights, from Flagler's own electrical plant, turned the Royal Palm into a fairyland that brought new hope to the burned-out city. Businesses rapidly rebuilt on what is now Flagler Street and the "Magic City" was back in business.

But Miami's troubles had only just begun. In the spring and summer of 1898, seventy-five hundred Spanish-American War troops came to a town that now had a population of twenty-five hundred people. The troops, miserable and bored, caused so many problems for the outnumbered Miamians that they called the situation the "Battle of Miami." The soldiers could not have agreed more. One soldier remarked that if he owned both Miami and hell, he would live in hell and rent out Miami. Fortunately for everyone, the war was brief and the troops quickly departed.

Just when things got back to normal, Miami faced an even more serious problem when, late in 1899, yellow fever broke out. For three months, no one was allowed in or out of town and more than two hundred people contracted the disease. To make matters worse, Miami experienced two more major fires during the quarantine. The second one burned down a large part of the new business district on what is now Flagler Street.

When one looks back on these early years, it is amazing that Miami made it at all. But from the beginning, Miami has always attracted a variety of people who have demonstrated an uncanny ability to overcome adversity and remain optimistic about the future. This was particularly apparent during the early years of the twentieth century when the "Magic City" lost its frontier, boom-time atmosphere and began to look like a respectable southern town. But beneath the "Miamah" facade,

Top right and above: Aventura is a booming community of new luxury condominiums. *Top left:* Turnberry Country Club, where afternoon tea is served traditionally and ceremoniously *(opposite, top right). Opposite, bottom:* Water Place is the fashionable mall of the Waterways, one of the new condominium complexes.

complete with Confederate monument on the courthouse lawn and Georgia-boy politicians, Miami was already developing its own constantly changing environment and personality.

The transformation of the land began in 1905 when the mayor declared a public holiday so the whole town could celebrate as the dredge dug the last few feet of Government Cut through the southern tip of Miami Beach. Four years later, the Everglades drainage program began—pushing the dry land westward from what is now Twenty-seventh Avenue and opening up miles of former wetlands to development.

Meanwhile, John Collins, a Quaker farmer from New Jersey who was trying to raise coconuts on Miami Beach, decided to give up on the trees and build a bridge to connect the ocean beach to Miami. He ran out of money when the bridge was half finished, and Fisher came to his rescue in return for property on the beach. In the summer of 1913, the bridge was opened and Fisher's transformation of a low-lying spit of sand and mangroves into Miami Beach began.

The first airplane came to Miami in 1911 in celebration of Miami's fifteenth birthday. Over five thousand turned out to see a Wright Brothers biplane take off from the old golf links (now the Metro-Justice Center). Within a few months, famous aviator Glen Curtiss opened a flying school in Miami, launching Miami's pivotal position as an aviation center. During World War I, the Navy took over Dinner Key and established one of the nation's first seaplane bases there.

By the time World War I broke out, Miami was already beginning to boom thanks to its first national advertising campaign: "It's Always June in Miami." To add to the tropical image, promoters encouraged everyone to dress in light-colored summer clothes and straw hats the year around (seventy years before "Miami Vice" reminded South Floridians of its tropical heritage). Millionaires were coming in, too. Many built pala-

tial estates on Brickell Avenue, in Coconut Grove, and on Miami Beach. The grandest of them all, James Deering's Villa Vizcaya, completed in 1916, set an architectural style that would be identified with South Florida in the years to come.

As soon as the war was over, Miamians rushed to pick up where they had left off in 1917. As the tempo increased, Miami's boundaries exploded, and by 1923, even the most high-blown predictions for Miami's future seemed to be coming true. In 1925, Miami's boom fever turned into an epidemic, and before it subsided the whole nation had contracted the disease.

Opposite, top left and bottom left: In addition to offering goods found in most flea markets, the Hialeah/Opa-Locka Outdoor Flea Market sells Caribbean foods and ingredients. *Opposite, top right:* A lake in Oleta River State Recreation Area is a cool haven on hot weekends. *Opposite, bottom and left:* Whether in downtown Opa-Locka or in residential North Miami, bright colors are a major part of the urban landscape.

West of town, George Merrick was selling "Coral Gables: Miami's Master Suburb." Merrick built a carefully planned community and then hired famous musicians like Jan Garber and Paul Whiteman and famous people like William Jennings Bryan to help him sell his "City Beautiful" to the world.

Even aviator Curtiss got in on the Boom. Along with rancher James Bright, he developed both Hialeah and Miami Springs. Curtiss also built the city of Opa-Locka with its Arabian Nights theme.

All around these major developments, individual parcels were rapidly being turned into subdivisions. The wild speculation was so intense that owners put "Not for Sale" signs on their property and Miami passed a law forbidding selling real estate on the street. It was not unusual for a new subdivision to sell out in a matter of hours as buyers literally threw their checks at the salesman, vying with each other for the privilege of purchasing land, by the foot or by the gallon—sight unseen.

In August 1925, the Florida East Coast Railroad announced

Aviator Glenn Curtiss, the developer of Opa-Locka, commissioned architect Berhardt Muller to build a theme city. Inspired by *The Arabian Nights*, Muller constructed a Moorish town with streets named after the characters in the stories.

a temporary freight embargo so the overburdened tracks could be rebuilt. This action cut off the lifeblood of materials. Builders hired anything afloat, including antique windjammers, to bring in the much-needed supplies. In early January 1926, the brigantine *Prinz Valdemar* capsized in the middle of Government Cut, blocking the entrance to Miami harbor for twenty-five days. By the time the old hulk was towed to shore, the red-hot Boom had turned ice-cold.

Just before midnight on September 17, the fury of a killer hurricane unleashed itself on an unsuspecting city. For eight sleepless hours, the storm raged. In the morning's gray light, the wind suddenly stopped, the clouds parted, and the people emerged from their homes to survey the damage. What most of them didn't know was that it was only the lull of the storm. Suddenly, without warning, the raging wind returned with even greater strength, stranding many unsuspecting residents outside.

Late in the afternoon of September 18 people emerged from their tattered homes through darkness and debris to view the sickening destruction. Miami had been brought to its knees. The Boom was over. The good times slipped away, and once again Miami faced disaster.

Refusing to give up, the University of Miami opened one month later, even though it had to use a half-completed apartment-hotel instead of its own building, which would remain unfinished for twenty years.

Even optimistic Miamians could not solve the serious problems facing the city. Developers abandoned their projects half completed, banks failed, and many fair-weather supporters promptly left town. But even in the darkest of days, all was not lost. In 1928, Pan American Airways moved to Miami from Key West. That same year Harold Pitcarin picked up the remains of Florida Airways, renamed it Pitcarin Airways, and

Hialeah, a mixed environment of light industry and inexpensive housing, is the site of the Miami Jai-Alai Fronton and the Amelia Earhart Park, with a large fishing lake. It is also home of the once world-famous Hialeah Park. Photographs of Winston Churchill and Harry S Truman, among others, are hung on the walls of the Hialeah Park Club House to remind visitors of the position the racetrack once occupied in the world of horse racing. Hialeah, which means "beautiful prairie" in the Seminole language, has a large colony of flamingos. The exotic birds were hatched and raised at the track.

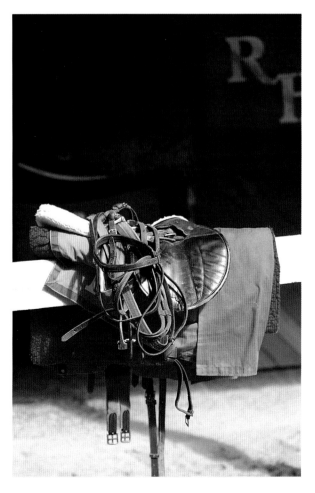

hired Eddie Rickenbacker to help run it. Two years later, the airline, renamed Eastern, began the first passenger service from Miami to points north.

After the stock market crash of 1929, the rest of the nation began to experience the kind of depression that Miami had already learned to tolerate. Shortly before his inauguration, Franklin Delano Roosevelt, who won the presidency in a landslide in 1932, came to Miami. While Roosevelt addressed eighteen thousand Miamians at Bayfront Park, an unemployed bricklayer, Guiseppe Zangara, fired five shots at the president-elect. Roosevelt was not hit but four others, including Mayor Anton Cermak of Chicago, went down. Rushed to Jackson Memorial Hospital, Cermak died on March 6. Justice was swift. Thirty-three days after Zangara almost changed the course of history, he was executed.

By the mid-1930s, while the rest of the nation was suffering in the slough of depression, Miami was showing signs of recovery. Pan American Airways, which had moved to Dinner Key (now Miami City Hall) from its Thirty-sixth Street Airport, had made Miami the jumping-off point for its international flights. The "Flying Clippers" were bringing in thousands of Latin tourists and advertising Miami as the "Gateway to the Americas."

The change from depression to recovery was especially apparent on Miami Beach. An increase in tourism prompted the construction of new hotels and apartment buildings with stark "moderne" lines that rose on Ocean Drive and Collins Avenue. In an effort to keep the tourists in Miami longer, a group of citizens organized a January event they called the Palm Fete. In 1934, they changed the name to the Orange Bowl Festival, which was played at a new stadium on January 1, 1935.

On December 7, 1941, the Sunday Miami Herald predicted

As night descends on Miami, a tugboat guides a Caribbean-bound ship through a drawbridge, down the Miami River.

that Miami would have the best tourist season in its history. By 2:30 p.m., however, everything had changed. The Japanese had bombed Pearl Harbor. Two months later, the reality of war hit hard when a German submarine torpedoed a tanker in full view of Miami shores. The locals panicked and the tourists scurried home.

Fear, patriotism, and empty hotels spurred Miamians into action. If the government could be convinced to turn Miami's empty hotels into major training centers, Miami and Miami Beach could be spared another depression. By the end of 1942, Miami boosters had convinced the government to take over 147 Miami Beach hotels as barracks for the Army Air Force's officers training school.

Meanwhile, the Navy moved its Gulf Sea Frontier headquarters to Miami and took over two entire floors of the city's only postboom skyscraper, the Alfred I. duPont Building, which they dubbed the U.S.S. *Neversink*. Eventually, the Navy, with the use of blimps stationed at Richmond Field (now the Metrozoo) and the sub-chaser school, housed north of Bayfront Park, ended the submarine menace off of Florida.

GIs, who got "sand in their shoes" while training here during the war, returned at its conclusion to Miami to stay. New subdivisions with rows of little pink, yellow, or blue stucco houses, a wrought-iron flamingo at each front door, sprung up everywhere, including Key Biscayne, which was soon connected to the mainland by causeway.

In the whirlwind of activity suddenly overtaking Miami, an incredible number of natural whirlwinds also blew into town. Between 1945 and 1950, eight hurricanes (the largest number in history) struck or grazed Miami. The second, in the fall of 1947, turned eighty percent of Dade and Broward counties into a lake. In response, the Army Corps of Engineers began a $208 million flood-control plan which created hundreds of thou-

sands of acres of new inhabitable land. In the years to come, over a million people would live on this reclaimed land. (The drainage, however, would have dire consequences on the future water supply.)

Throughout its history, Miami had done just about anything to please the tourists. This included being labeled the "leakiest" spot in America during Prohibition and putting up with many unsavory types who were drawn to Miami's look-the-other-way attitude toward illegal gambling. In the 1950s, a group of Miami citizens decided enough was enough and led a campaign to clean up the city. Before it was over, Senate crime-fighter Estes Kefauver was brought to town, many public officials were indicted, and most, if not all, of South Florida's gambling casinos were closed.

On the first day of 1959, it seemed that the typical New Year's Eve celebration was continuing into the next day. The cheering crowds were not celebrating the new year, however. They were celebrating the fall of Cuban dictator Fulgencio Batista and the rise to power of a thirty-two-year-old revolu-

The Miami River was first settled by Native Americans. In the late 1800s, the first Anglos in Miami built their homes along the river. The early settlers' cottages are still inhabited by river enthusiasts. Fort Dallas, now painted bright yellow, was the home of one of Henry Flagler's workers. Professional fishing boats unload their catches at the fisheries along the river, attracting flocks of pelicans. Recreational fishing boats and luxury yachts leave the large shipyards located upriver.

tionary named Fidel Castro. No one in Miami dreamed that his revolution would change the course of Miami history as well as Cuban history. As Castro showed his true colors, a nonstop stream of exiles flowed into Miami. By the summer of 1960, the stream became a flood as six planes a day arrived from Havana. For the most part, the exiles were destitute and received modest assistance from the U.S. government ($100 a month and food stamps). Until 1961, however, most believed that it would be a temporary exile and the Cubans would soon return home. The Central Intelligence Agency,

A container yard, a cargo port, and smaller loading docks serve the large number of cargo ships and freighters that travel up and down the river. Tugboat pilots must perform extraordinary feats to maneuver the large cargo ships among the loading and unloading vessels. Well-worn ships daily leave the Miami River for Haiti, overloaded with second-hand bicycles, old refrigerators, mattresses, large plastic containers, and other household items. Sponge boats come to small factories to unload raw sponges caught offshore and cleaned in Biscayne Bay by the Rickenbacker Causeway.

which organized a brigade of exiles to free Cuba, encouraged this feeling. When the April 1961 invasion of Cuba failed, because the United States called off its promised air support, Miami's refugee community was devastated and believed that the government, which had recruited, trained, and funded the freedom fighters, had betrayed them.

A year later, Miami was again in the middle of the storm when it was discovered that the Russians had been building missile pads in Cuba. Not since the German submarine scare of 1942 had Miamians been so frightened. The immediate crisis was averted when Nikita Khrushchev agreed to remove the missiles if the United States promised not to invade Cuba or allow anyone else to. For the first time, Miami's one hundred thousand Cuban refugees realized that a long time would pass before they could return home—if ever.

In the late 1960s, a Cuban refugee arrived in Miami every seven minutes. The refugees were processed in the old Miami News Tower, which they renamed the Freedom Tower, Miami's own Statue of Liberty. By the end of the decade, four hundred thousand Cuban refugees were living in Dade County.

Looking back on the 1960s, it is clear that the incredible combination of events that took place would greatly impact Miami's future. At the same time the Cubans were pouring into Miami to start their lives over, the 1964 Civil Rights Acts changed the rules for everyone else. In the next decade, Miami's schools and public facilities were desegregated, and many other previously accepted practices that segregated the races were relegated to history. The change in law, however, did not bring the changes in society that many hoped would occur. The Cubans, eager for any work, quickly supplanted many of the black workers, creating serious problems for the blacks, who had new expectations for the future. Misunderstanding, frustration, and broken promises added to the frustra-

First Union

tion that erupted into serious problems for Miami.

Despite these many new problems, the 1970s were filled with mostly sunny days. In 1972, the Miami Dolphins succeeded in bringing the diverse community together as the team won seventeen straight games, including a Super Bowl championship. Likewise, Miami Dade Community College was growing with the community and providing educational opportunities for everyone. The skyline added new skyscrapers for the first time in years. Even a serious recession at the middle of the decade did not dampen the community's pride.

To those who did not know Miami's history, 1980 appeared to be the worst year Miami had ever known. In January, the popular black superintendent of schools was indicted and later convicted of theft of school property. In May, blacks in Liberty City and other parts of the city rioted after a Tampa jury acquitted the policemen who killed Arthur McDuffie, a black businessman. Although the smoke and flames were extinguished, a heavy cloud of despair hung over the city.

Brickell Avenue, Miami's banking center, is also the city's architectural showplace. Office towers are concentrated at the north end of the avenue. Exclusive condominium towers occupy the south end.

South Florida's vast shoreline and proximity to the bubble and boil of Latin American and Caribbean politics proved inviting to political and economic refugees as well as drug traffickers from many countries. Thousands of Haitians in makeshift boats landed on South Florida shores. Despite their best efforts, Coast Guard patrols could not begin to seal off South Florida's coast.

When Castro announced that Cubans who wished to emigrate could leave, thousands of Cuban-Americans sailed to Cuba's Mariel Harbor to transport their countrymen to Miami. Miami braced itself to handle one hundred twenty-five thousand more refugees, many with dubious pasts.

For a time, the combination of events seemed to overwhelm

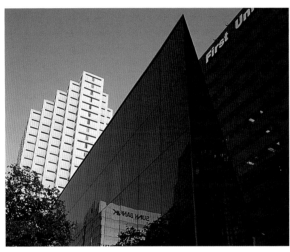

The downtown Miami architecture plays with the sunlight. Reflections are everywhere. *Opposite, top left:* Beyond the Capital Bank Tower, the Palace, Villa Regina, Imperial, and Atlantis condominiums display the creativity of Arquitectonica, one of Miami's premier architectural firms. *Opposite, top right, and below:* The Atlantis, with a palm tree shading a hot tub in the middle of the building, is the most photographed piece of architecture in Miami.

the city. Winds of rage and fear, as strong as a hurricane, swirled in the midst of the maelstrom.

Miamians also rolled up their sleeves. Before the 1980s came to an end Miami's skyline had been transformed, but other needed changes were more elusive. Three major national writers penned books on Miami. T. D. Allman, author of *Miami, City of the Future,* seemed to understand the city the best when he wrote that Miami was in the middle of experiencing and dealing with issues that the rest of the nation had only begun to understand. Miami had an opportunity. If it could resolve its problems, it could set an example for the rest of the nation, which would experience some of the same situations in the next century.

In short, Miami's history proves that a diverse group of people who came from someplace else have developed an uncanny ability to overcome adversity and adapt to change. Nothing in Miami's past proves this better than the history of the last thirty years. The transformation of Miami from a second-class metropolis into a first-class international city has been nothing short of miraculous. Thriving amid change is what Miami's magic is all about. ❖

Left and above: The Villa Regina. Agam was hired to design its facade. *Below left:* The Imperial. *Below right:* The Palace. *Bottom:* Villa Regina fountain and Palace swimming pool.

Key Biscayne, an island just minutes away from downtown and Brickell Avenue, has preserved its peaceful, tropical island feeling. Bill Baggs Cape Florida State Recreation Area lies at the southern end of the island and Crandon Park occupies the northern end. Between these parks, a few hotels and condominiums face east to the Atlantic Ocean, and secluded homes face west to Biscayne Bay.

Weekends the year around bring Miamians, especially Hispanics, to the white sand beaches of Biscayne Bay. Families picnicking with their children prefer the parks' beaches, while couples and young singles concentrate around the hotels.

Key Biscayne offers all the pleasures of an exotic tropical island: palm trees, white sand, ocean view, swimming pools, volleyball games, and the deep blue of cloudless skies. It is also the home of bankers, lawyers, business executives, and doctors, whose offices are located minutes away on the other side of Biscayne Bay. Tourists and "snowbirds," or winter residents, join in the outdoor activities in winter and spring.

Vizcaya, an Italian Renaissance villa and gardens, was built in 1916 by James Deering on the mainland shore of Biscayne Bay in Coconut Grove. Today it is a decorative art museum, and the setting of several annual festivals, including the Cornucopia of the Arts, Italian Renaissance Fair, and Beethoven's Birthday Celebration. The Vizcayans, an organization of volunteers, are responsible for raising funds and promoting the museum, and the villa and gardens. A major fundraiser is the elegant, annual Vizcayan Ball.

Coconut Grove is an eclectic community. Its two prestigious yacht clubs informally oversee sailing in Biscayne Bay. Elegant homes with both sailboats and speed-boats border the waterways. Bohemi-ans, intellectuals, artists, and young pro-fessionals frequent the numerous restaurants, cafes, nightclubs, and fashionable boutiques.

After the coral was quarried for the houses of Coral Gables, developer George Merrick had the quarry turned into the Venetian Pool. It is still enjoyed as a swimming pool by the community, and is favored as a background for fashion shoots.

Women have played an important part in the development of Miami. We owe the survival of Miami to Julia Tuttle's foresight. She saw in Henry Flagler the person needed to open this new-found land to the rest of the country. As John Sewell writes in his *Miami Memoirs*, "Julia Tuttle gave the land, and Henry Flagler the money." *Opposite*: Marjory Stoneman Douglas, another woman of foresight. No mention of the preservation of the Everglades can be made without crediting her. At 101-years-old and partially blind, she is currently writing another book. *Above left*: Pueblo Hotel Retirement Home in Miami Springs. *Above*: Coral Gables City Hall. *Center left*: The original Coral Gables home where George Merrick spent his adolescence. *Bottom left*: The new Metro-Dade Police Headquarters.

Greater Miami stretches south from Aventura, the growing condominium complex, to Homestead, the agricultural center. Downtown Homestead is the site of the annual Homestead Rodeo and parade. Greenhouses and farms surround the community.

THE MICCOSUKEES BY STEPHEN TIGER

There is much common ground between the Miccosukees, the Seminoles, and the tribes of the Creek Confederacies. Yet the Miccosukees are an independent tribe with a history of their own. We were originally part of the Creek Confederacy, with a history in Florida that dates back prior to the 1600s. Verbal accounts of our history have been passed down through the centuries by elders in our native language, Mikasuki. But most of these stories have not been translated or written. The Miccosukees came to settle in what is now known as Dade County in the mid-1800s as a result of the many wars and hardships brought on by the non-Indian settlers who staked claim to Florida.

The Miccosukees have an airboat concession for tourist rides. Here, one of the drivers rests on the safety railing of his airboat. In the Everglades, the airboat is the most efficient way of transportation, though it is also extremely noisy. The airboat is powered by an airplane engine and propeller mounted on the back and surrounded by a metal cage for safety. The flat bottom allows the boat to skim over the shallow wetlands of the Everglades.

The Miccosukees are essentially a nonmaterialistic society whose beliefs stem from the earth and Mother Nature. It is for this reason that our tribal leaders decided to stay virtually isolated in the Everglades and refuse any offers for assistance from the federal or state governments. It wasn't until the land we called home was declared a national park and we were once again asked to relocate that our elders decided it was time to officially take a stand.

My father, William Buffalo Tiger, was selected to represent the tribe in all of the negotiations necessary to become a federally recognized tribe. Initially the U.S. government resisted our attempts, so the tribe decided to take an Indian delegation to Fidel Castro in Cuba, where they were officially recognized as a new Indian nation and even offered a place to live. This was apparently the straw that broke the camel's back, for Washing-

For the Miccosukee children, school attendance is not mandatory; however, the tribe school is well attended. *Opposite, bottom:* A group of young students watches a video of their performance in a school play. *Opposite, top:* On Mother's Day the schoolchildren invite their mothers and grandmothers for a celebration lunch. *Below, center and bottom:* Stephen Tiger rehearses with band members in his apartment away from the Everglades, but his days are spent at the tribe's administrative complex and village where his paintings are displayed.

ton then agreed to take our situation seriously. On January 11, 1962, the Miccosukee constitution was approved by the Secretary of the Interior and the tribe was officially organized.

The constitution was designed to help us grow without losing our traditions. Parents can still elect to teach their children at home instead of forcing them into a non-Indian school system. Mikasuki is still the first language spoken. All through the 1960s, our tribe prospered, opening a school, a community gymnasium, a restaurant, an outpatient clinic, and an administrative complex.

I myself have been raised in both worlds, going to school in Miami before there were schools on the reservation. I did spend most of my childhood in the Everglades. It seems that being an artist comes naturally to Miccosukee people. The women who make beautiful, brightly colored patchwork, dolls, beadwork, and baskets served as an inspiration for me in both my art and my music. I have tried to use these means to help break down the barriers created by stereotypical images of Indians. I have written several songs about my tribe and have tried to portray them in my paintings. In 1975 we had our first official annual music and crafts festival using the arts as a positive communications vehicle between Indian and non-Indian people. We are now in our seventeenth year and have continued not only to raise funds for our education department but have succeeded in providing an event where all the ethnic communities of South Florida can come together to showcase their individual contributions to Miami.

In 1978, we claimed ownership of all lands south and west of Lake Okeechobee including Ft. Myers and Naples. To represent our interest in the United States, we officially opened an embassy in Miami in November 1984.

Some people may say we are a very bold and feisty tribe. Like the mouse that roared, we think of ourselves as strong,

even though we number less than four hundred enrolled members. We know that in order to survive as an Indian nation, we must teach our people to overcome any obstacles that fall in our path, as our ancestors did, and to learn to live in harmony with the many new cultures that share South Florida. ❖

Along the Tamiami Trail is Coopertown, home of Jesse Kennon and his family. They operate an airboat concession and a restaurant. His airboats have been used in movies and TV shows.

Flamingos and alligators are the two animals that most represent Florida. Alligators are found at Metrozoo and Seaquarium, but the Everglades is their natural habitat. Airboat pilots point them out to visitors and can also find alligator eggs that have not yet hatched.

The Everglades, one of America's true wilderness areas, is a very tenuous ecosystem. Every year acres are cleared by fire. Much of the water that feeds the Everglades has been diverted for agricultural and city use, leaving expanses of dry brush and grasses. The alligator's natural habitat is slowly disappearing.

Purple gallinules *(opposite, top left)*; common gallinules *(above)*; and snowy egrets *(opposite, bottom and left)* are common sights in the Everglades. However, one has to take to the back trails to encounter otters *(bottom)* or owls.

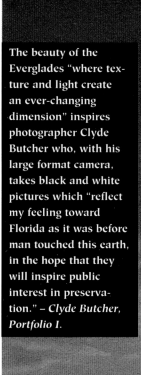

The beauty of the Everglades "where texture and light create an ever-changing dimension" inspires photographer Clyde Butcher who, with his large format camera, takes black and white pictures which "reflect my feeling toward Florida as it was before man touched this earth, in the hope that they will inspire public interest in preservation." – *Clyde Butcher, Portfolio I.*

MIAMI IN BLACK BY DR. MARVIN DUNN

There are many shades of black in Miami: ethnic shades, economic shades, religious shades, and political shades, among others. There is, therefore, no such thing as the "Black Community" of Miami. There are many black communities in Miami. Indeed, black Miami is composed of many kinds of black people with quite different experiences, priorities, and perceptions. Except for the commonality of their skin color, they are as different among themselves as they are from the whites and browns who have enveloped them.

With the arrival of Henry Flagler's railroad in Miami in 1896, farms began to sprout up, almost overnight, along its path as the railroad plunged southward toward the sea. With the coming of the railroad, Dade County's economic base was suddenly expanded. Black labor was very much in demand for the developing farms and businesses. Blacks were needed as common laborers to help clear the land and to lay out the streets for the new city. With the tremendous market for common laborers, well over a third of the new residents arriving in Miami during the actual building of the city were black. On July 28, 1896, when the city of Miami was founded, 162 of the 368 people who voted to establish the city were black. Indeed, Miami's first registered voter was a black man.

The Orange Blossom Classic Parade and Festival, held every fall, is an important celebration in Liberty City. With this parade and the Sunstreet Festival, the black community is showcased to the rest of Miami.

The demand for low-skilled labor was met successfully by blacks from the Bahamas and by black laborers who had worked on the railroad and now needed permanent work. The labor demand was also met by those blacks who had been pushed farther south on the Florida peninsula as a result of the great freeze of 1894-95, which devastated the agricultural industry of the southeastern United States. Their usefulness in

The Orange Blossom Classic Parade. Families line Seventh Avenue between Northwest Fifty-seventh and Seventy-first streets to watch their children march in the bands or to see the many floats filled with Orange Blossom royalty.

agriculture assured, blacks began to carve out a niche for themselves in the burgeoning tourist economy after the turn of the century.

Bahamian blacks started to arrive in force in Miami in the late 1800s as the city was in the birth process. In the early years they outnumbered native-born blacks in the city of Miami. Their influence is still lyrically woven into the simple yet enduring architecture of some old black sections of Miami, especially in the Coconut Grove and Overtown areas.

Each summer the Bahamian influence erupts in sound, color, and culinary bliss in Black Grove's annual Goombay Festival. Goombay is a widespread celebration, of African origin, which is held in many parts of the black Caribbean and in the Bahamas. It was imported to the Black Grove by the early black Bahamian settlers, many of whom returned to the island at Goombay time. In the Black Grove's Goombay, Grand Avenue becomes a swirling, undulating mass of black, brown, and white, mingling, sweating, dancing, and eating together. It is Miami at its best.

Many of the early arriving blacks from the lower southern states and the Bahamas settled in the area of Miami that was specifically established as the segregated living quarters for blacks. The main "colored" section was in the northwest section of the city, on the other side (west) of the railroad track and opposite downtown. It was known as Colored Town, and later as Overtown or Culmer. In the early 1900s, as Miami arrived on the national scene, black Miami was pulsating to its own beat, and it was quickly filling up with people. The culture of black Miami flowed along northwest Second Avenue, originally known as Avenue G during the Flagler era. Blacks simply called it "the Avenue" and everyone knew where and what it was.

Because of the high quality of entertainment to be found

Top right and above: **The Orange Blossom Classic Parade features bands such as world renowned Florida A&M University's Marching Band. This band has appeared in parades throughout the United States and Europe.**

there, during the 1930s and 1940s, Second Avenue between Sixth and Tenth streets gained a national and international reputation as Miami's "Little Broadway." It was also known as "The Strip" and "The Great Black Way." For over three decades, it became *the* place to be seen in black Miami. In its heyday, no self-respecting black person would be caught on the Avenue without being clean shaven, well dressed, and quite prim and proper, even during the week.

Because they were not allowed to spend the night in white sections of town, black entertainers who had performed on Miami Beach during this period would head to Overtown's nightclubs and hotels after their last performances on the Beach. There, in Colored Town, the real action would start, often lasting until daybreak. Many greats performed regularly, including Count Basie, Ella Fitzgerald, Cab Calloway, Josephine Baker, Billie Holiday, Sammy Davis, Jr., the Ink Spots, Louis "Satchmo" Armstrong, Nat King Cole, B. B. King, Aretha Franklin, Dionne Warwick, and Bessie Smith.

Overtown's success in the 1930s through the 1950s was not limited to local black patronage. White tourists and residents frequented the area for entertainment, to sample soul food, and to listen to gospel music. The money spent by tourists and visitors contributed to the economic stability of the black business community.

Majestically, in the center of all this, stood the Lyric Theater. Built by a wealthy black businessman, Gedar Walker, it first opened in 1919, serving as a movie house and social center. Even with the advent of talkies, the Lyric showed only silent pictures. In addition, vaudevilles, concerts, dramas, political meetings, boxing matches, rallies, beauty pageants, club activities, and school plays were held there.

The Lyric stands today as one of the few remaining testaments to the grandeur of Overtown in its starlit zenith. For a

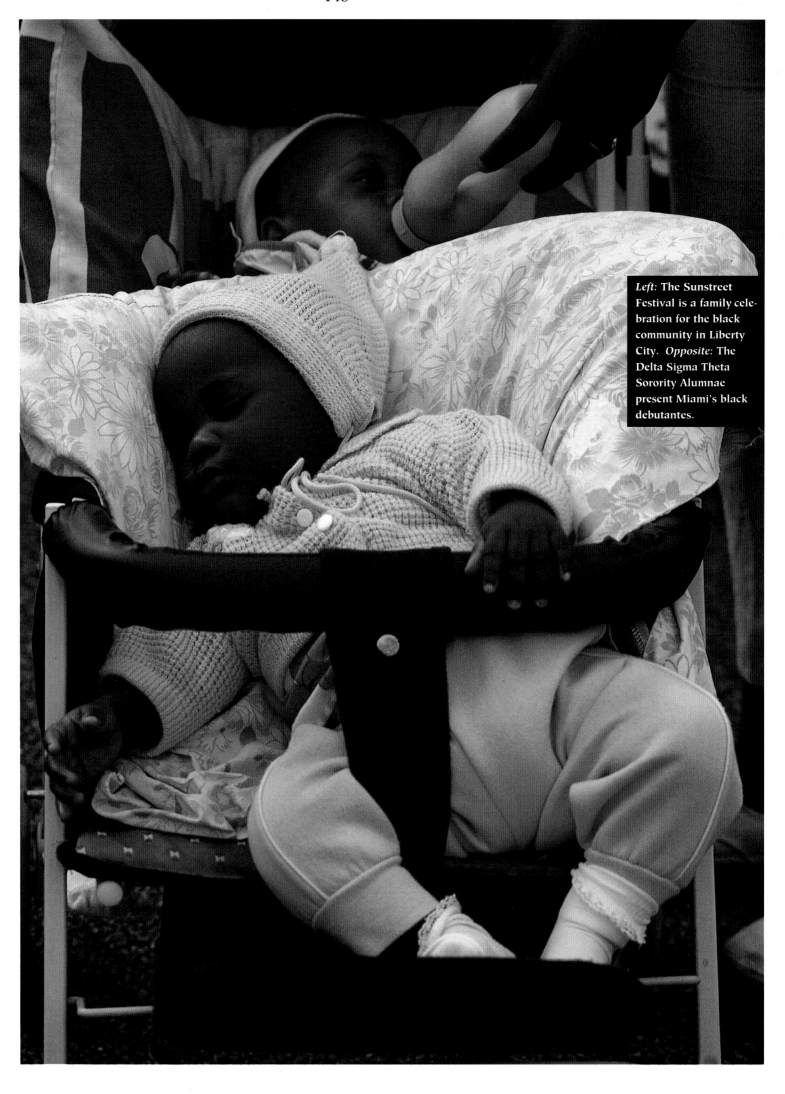

Left: The Sunstreet Festival is a family celebration for the black community in Liberty City. *Opposite:* The Delta Sigma Theta Sorority Alumnae present Miami's black debutantes.

while it stood vacant; then, in 1960, it was converted to a church. For several years after its use as a church, it stood vacant and in disrepair. In 1990, the building was starting to be restored as a part of the renaissance of Overtown that is underway.

In the late 1950s and early 1960s, Overtown's vibrancy became snuffed out. Desegregation, urban renewal, and construction of two expressways altered the character of the neighborhood. Black ownership of hotels, nightclubs, and other places of entertainment declined. These changes also meant the demise of "Little Broadway."

Following years of strident opposition by whites to black attempts to break out of the traditional black sections of the city, and as a result of court rulings on housing discrimination dating to the late 1940s, in the early 1950s the northwest portion of Dade County, beyond Colored Town and Liberty City, was opened up to blacks. Like birds uncaged, they flew northward to the county line by the mid-1980s. With the mass exodus of much of its middle and upper classes, the older traditional black sections of the city declined rapidly.

The civil rights movement did not bypass Miami. Beginning in the mid-1940s, civil rights agitations by blacks culminated in a flurry of court and street actions to accelerate the social integration of blacks into mainstream Miami. Dr. Martin Luther King visited Miami many times during the civil rights era and had several close black friends in Miami. The King legacy is still ablaze in Miami.

Miami's lifeblood for much of her existence flowed to and from the north. Today the city's heart pumps southward toward Central and South America and, as it always has, toward Cuba and Haiti in the Caribbean.

Since the 1960s but particularly in the 1980s, Miami's black population has exploded with the influx of blacks from Central

The Sunstreet Festival lasts one week. Besides including a parade, it is an occasion for the community to display the goods sold in the stores. *Opposite, bottom:* Architectural detail of a shopping complex, a recent addition to the community in Little Haiti.

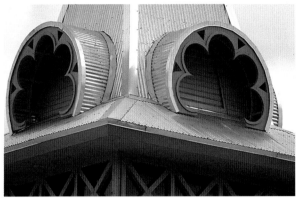

and South America and from the Caribbean, particularly Cuba and Haiti. There are also a considerable number of blacks in Miami of Jamaican descent.

Thus, the linkage between blacks in Miami and Africa may be, by way of the Caribbean, much stronger and more apparent than it is between blacks in other American cities and Africa. This can be seen in the structures, patterns, and colors that define black Miami today.

And it can be heard when the people speak. In addition to standard black English, black language in Miami is richly varied in intonations and cadences from Jamaica, Haiti, Cuba, the Bahamas, and a dozen other places with recent and direct ties to the motherland.

Some of the most dramatic architectural transformations in Miami from white to black are occurring in the formerly all-white Edison area, northwest of downtown. Although initially settled by native-born blacks, this area first attracted many of the Haitians who began arriving in Miami in the late 1970s and early 1980s. By 1990 Miami had yet another intact, black ethnic community: "Little Haiti." Little Haiti supports an entire community infrastructure, including growing businesses and churches, schools, nightlife, and many Haitian restaurants. It is unique.

For the Haitians, Miami represented hope and a fresh second beginning in life. With their coming, Miami was given new, warm, and soaring colors, and a deep taste of Africa. The city's most direct link with Africa was irrevocably established.

Although signs of blight are very apparent in the poorer sections of black Miami, a prevailing, persistent beat of optimism struggles to be heard. Rooted in the turbulent days of Miami's civil rights era, it is an optimism that has not been entirely misplaced.

There are many misconceptions about black Miami. One of

Overtown was settled by black railroad workers in the pioneer days. This wall mural by Purvis Young conveys the legacy and some of the energy of the community's past. In the 1940s and 1950s, it was known as Little Broadway because of the Lyric Theater and jazz clubs. In recent times, it has had difficulty maintaining an identity. To overcome this hardship, the Historic Overtown Village planners are working toward revitalizing the community.

these is that all, or most, black Miamians are poor and have been muscled out of the job market by newly arriving immigrants, black, white, and particularly, brown. This has been a lingering legacy from Miami's time of fire: the 1980s, when the city was rocked by a series of racial disturbances. Yet there has not been any compelling evidence to support such a view.

Since 1980, Dade County's black population growth has stabilized at approximately twenty percent of the total population of the county, effectively keeping pace with the growth of the Hispanic population. This is largely due to the considerable immigration of foreign-born blacks.

In the late 1980s, there were more than three hundred fifty thousand blacks in Dade County. An assessment of their current status reveals a mixed picture. On the one hand, one in five adult blacks fails to complete high school. About fifty percent of black workers are employed in lower paying, generally blue- and pink-collar occupations. The median income of black families in the early 1980s was about sixty-three percent of the median income of white families, and about sixty percent of black births were to unwed mothers, compared with thirteen percent of white births.

Yet there were many encouraging signs. Blacks made giant strides in closing the gap in education attainment. The median years of school completed by the blacks lagged behind the median for the whites by only half a year. Ten years previously the lag was two and one-half years.

Blacks enrolled in college at an increasing rate. The 1980 figures showed one in five adult blacks enrolled in higher education compared with only one in ten in 1970. Blacks filled about twenty percent of the new jobs added to the Dade County economy in recent years and were able for the first time in the 1980s to capture a fair percentage of the higher paying white-collar jobs.

Top: A mural in Little Haiti. *Bottom:* Miami Arena in Overtown is the home of the basketball franchise Miami Heat. *Opposite, top:* The Lyric Theater in Overtown is awaiting renovation. *Opposite, center:* The Cultural Art Center in Liberty City. *Opposite, bottom:* A Rastafarian merchant and customer in Liberty City.

Black employment in many white-collar occupations doubled and, in some instances, tripled in the 1970s. In 1980, blacks held 13 percent of the fast-growing professional, speciality, and technical occupations, compared with only seven percent ten years prior.

Black families in Dade, unlike their counterparts nationwide, began to close the income gap in the 1970s. After adjusting for inflation, the median income of black families in the Miami area rose by a modest seven percent; the incomes of other groups were virtually unchanged, increasing by two percent or less. There are signs, too, of an emerging black affluent class. Black families with incomes of $35,000 or more doubled in the course of the last decade.

Black Miami's slow climb into the mainstream has been helped by many of the community's concerned white and Hispanic citizens. White Miamians marched with blacks during the civil rights struggle. Forceful and responsible whites have called upon the larger community for the inclusion of blacks in the economic mainstream of the community. In the aftermath of the 1980 riot, the Chamber of Commerce raised more than $6 million, which was used for assistance to black businesses in recovering from the effects of the disturbance. Influential Hispanic organizations have been involved in direct job outreach efforts in black Miami. It can hardly be contended that all is well with blacks in Miami. Still, black Miami is hardly on the verge of collapse. It lives. ❖

AMERICANS LOVE TO EAT HERE BY DIANA MONTANE

Food is the great equalizer here, the good seal of acclimatization into what Miamians proudly hail as their multicultural stew.

Find a Miamian who doesn't know Cuban rice and beans, Spanish paella or *tres leches,* the rich Nicaraguan dessert named after the three kinds of milk from which it is made, and you'll have stumbled into a recent transplant from the North, or a potential escapee to a less threatening country "where they speak English."

Although upscale Anglo Miamians pride themselves in their acquired multiethnic taste buds, they're also ashamed to admit they can't really penetrate the mango-vine that grows like an exotic, if bothersome, weed underneath the savory cloud of kitchen smoke.

Wolfson Campus of Miami-Dade Community College presents many community-related events of varying duration that emphasize the ethnic diversity of the population. The college endeavors to stimulate the intellect by offering programs such as the Miami Book Fair International, Black Heritage Month, and Hispanic Heritage Month. It stimulates the palate with such celebrations as Hispanic Heritage Month's Paella Night. Participants sample paellas from various restaurants, cooked in immense pans over outdoor log fires.

For that, you have to speak Spanish.

The Cuba–United States ties have solidified since the nineteenth-century Spanish colonization on the island. Since then, exile has become an occupational hazard as well as an emblem of cachet. Cubans, first fleeing from the colony, and then from corrupt republican governments, went to Miami, New York, and Key West to establish enclaves from which to reconquer their land.

The 1960s witnessed the first mass exodus of an entrepreneurial class to Miami, which was able to enter the mainstream and stake high claims in it within a decade. Soon the emporium was sprawled out like a string of exotic signs proclaiming the hyperbolic best in food, appliances, jewelry, and even statuary and herbs, all

along what was once referred to as "The Trail" or "Tamiami," newly baptized with the Spanish surname for Southwest Eighth Street: Calle Ocho.

The city celebrates its ethnicity in a series of festivals, and its beat vibrates for miles during the second week in March, when the Latin community throws the biggest block party in Hispanic U.S.A., known simply as "Calle Ocho." The Kiwanis Club of Little Havana began sponsoring the event in 1978 in the spirit of a grateful fiesta for their Anglo hosts and neighbors. They expected ten thousand guests, and a hundred thousand showed up.

Since then, over one million Miamians and visitors flock to the twenty-three block radius emanating from Eighth Street, link on to the world's longest conga line, and elbow their way past hundreds of booths serving anything from hot dogs to *fritas,* the spicy Cuban counterpart of the burger, and past hundreds of stages where musicians play everything there is to dance.

In 1982, "Carnaval Miami" was instituted as part of "Calle Ocho," and fashioned after the famous carnivals in Cuba. With typical poetic penchant for continuity, the first carnival king was the first Cuban exile to "make good" in America, Desi Arnaz.

South West Eighth Street, Tamiami Trail, and Calle Ocho are names for the same avenue that crosses the Florida peninsula, from Little Havana on the east coast to the Everglades on the west coast. The first few eastern miles pass through Little Havana. *Opposite, top left:* The colorful map of Cuba on the Edificio José Martí. *Opposite, top right:* The monument A los Mártires de la Brigada de Asalto. *Opposite, center left:* The El Crédito cigar factory. *Opposite, bottom left and right:* Cafeterias that serve strong Cuban café. *Top left:* A botánica selling religious statues. *Bottom left:* During festivals, street vendors offer various foods.

By the time the first Cuban exiles moved out of the area called Little Havana near downtown Miami and into plush residential suburbs, the old empty buildings were turned into tenements for the new immigrants—successive waves of Cuban exiles, and Central and South Americans.

Miami's population is close to two million, and half of it is

Cuban traditions are still strong in Little Havana. Merchandise in the stores ranges from fruit-flavored ice cream, to papier-maché piñatas to fill with candy for children's parties, to love or saint's sprays. At home, religion is expressed by the numerous santuarios in the gardens. Celebration for "Los Quince," when a young woman turns fifteen, always brings a photo session in a stunning white dress, and most of the time means a large party.

Cuban, followed in decreasing numbers by Nicaraguans, Colombians, Salvadorans, Dominicans, Puerto Ricans, and "Others," which include a small aristocratic elite from Argentina and Peru numbering close to twenty thousand.

Next to the Cuban food chain, the Nicaraguan is the most visible, and the Nicaraguan community most like the Cuban in clannishness, political infrastructure, and sense of national pride. One Honduran was heard complaining about a Nicaraguan by saying, "These Nicaraguans . . . they think they're Cuban."

Miami's bad press, which proliferated in the 1980s as a result of the crime spree that followed the Mariel boatlift and the cocaine wars, eventually shifted like the coral sands of the city's foundations. The "Marielitos" assimilated within the Cuban-American mainstream within a decade, and the cartels set up shop elsewhere.

Colombians, however, still feel defensive about the scarlet C that was pinned on them by other Latins. One Colombian reporter remembers being asked by a car dealer why she didn't have instant cash. "You're Colombian, aren't you?" was the rhetorical invective.

Colombians now own radio stations and operate local newspapers, and vote in absentia at the elegant Colombian consulate in staid and affluent Coral Gables, in gatherings that often include art auctions and cultural activities.

As with other Latin American cities, there are polarities of wealth and poverty at both ends of the spectrum, with illegal aliens now filling the maintenance jobs once held by the Cubans, who quickly adopted the Calvinistic work ethic though maintaining the language of the heart.

Cubans set the pace of the Latin community but also set themselves apart. Mostly of Spanish descent, their restaurants are mostly Spanish in flavor and decor. Hispanic Heritage

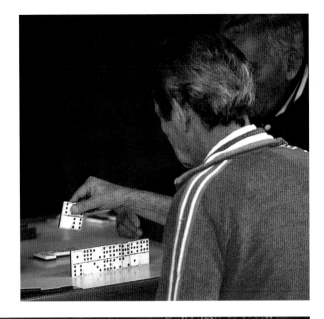

At Maximo Gomez Park, Cuban men, smoking huge cigars and generally speaking only Spanish, meet every day to play chess and dominos.

month, held every October, celebrates the arrival of the three Spanish ships on America's shores with an array of folkloric dances and lots and lots of food, including a paella so big it has to be stirred with oars.

There is no mistaking Miami for any other city with a heavy "Latino" population. "I'm not a Latino," one Cuban actor remarked, "I don't come from Latonia. I'm a Cuban."

A well-known ethnologist summed up the Cuban phenomenon in Miami: "We're a curious mixture. We're more American than anyone, more Spanish than anyone, and more African than anyone, and live happily with that dissonance."

Although it's true that Cubans readily embrace the American way of life, they're also zealous in their defense of what they consider to be symbols of their adoptive country, as witnessed by this bumper sticker on the Cadillac of a Cuban-American psychologist: "Flag Burners Beware: If I See You Burning the Flag of My Country, I Will Use My Freedom of Expression to Adjust Your Attitude."

All of this is perceived by Anglos as the tip of an encroaching monolith, but as the city grows, it develops a plurality of vision, and the exile community sheds its conservative protective hide to take on other colorations. The official pastime is finding newer and newer metaphors for what categorically refuses to be pegged, or to melt into a pot.

Among themselves, these separate communities who share a common language also find a common ground: music and art. Miami is a mecca for the amalgamation of Latin sounds, where everything passes for salsa, from Caribbean flamenco to Cuban *son*, to Dominican merengue and Colombian *cumbia*.

It is also rapidly becoming one of the strongest centers for Latin art in the United States, producing unique forms which are born of European traditions, bred with magic realism, and raised in the city and thus reflective of its ever-changing nature.

165

Inspired by the Giralda Tower of Seville Cathedral, architects Schultz and Weaver built the Biltmore Hotel and Country Club in the mid-1920s, as part of George Merrick's development of Coral Gables. During World War II, it was turned into a veteran's hospital. It was restored as a hotel in the 1980s.

Still, "Americans love to eat here." That is the passport into the Anglo mainstream, and the one conversation piece in which all groups participate.

And everyone, but everyone, passes through, or must be taken to, Versailles, the center of social hubbub on Calle Ocho, and the restaurant that serves the best and most plentiful Cuban food in town. Decorated in a kitschy Cuban rococo style and flanked by mirrors all around, Versailles is probably the best metaphor for a city that feeds itself off reflections of itself, and whose Latin denizens eye one another with unrelenting attention.

One cultural observer pointed out the pattern whereby immigrant groups engender businesses: shops and restaurants by the first and second generation, and art, perhaps, by the third and the fourth.

For Miami, the future is already here. It's all done with mirrors. ❖

Coral Gables, founded by George Merrick in the 1920s, is not only a suburb with luxurious residences, but a city with multinational corporations and the home of several consulates and trade commissions. The business and cultural activity has prompted the addition of several large hotels. *Left and bottom:* Hyatt Regency, Coral Gables. *Opposite, top left and right:* Hotel Place St. Michel. *Opposite, center left:* Hyatt Regency, Coral Gables. *Opposite, bottom left and right:* Biltmore Hotel.

Coral Gables. Lush vegetation and elegant houses follow George Merrick's dream of building a "City Beautiful." Among his plans was a village concept, each village having a different architecture. Shutters can be seen on the windows of the French Village, City Style; whereas red tile was used on the roofs of the French Village, Country Style.

Coral Gables is a mix of
many periods and styles.
George Merrick's dream
houses and majestic old
banyan trees *(left)*,
peaceful canals *(bottom
left)*, and Allen's Drugs
(bottom right) where
time stopped in the
1950s, contrast with the
new Coral Gables.
*Opposite, bottom and
top left:* Miracle Center,
an ultra-modern
shopping mall.
Opposite, top right: The
Coconut Grove Conven-
tion Center.

Miamians spend weekends at celebrations, events, festivals, parades, and fairs. The largest festivity is Carnaval Miami. Calle Ocho Open House possibly attracts the largest crowd. Paseo is the most colorful. Floats and street dancers parade past the crowd lining Flagler and Southwest First streets again and again.

Speedboat and sail-boat races are common sights in Biscayne Bay and along Government Cut. Away from the bay and ocean, events range from high stakes horse racing in the Breeder's Cup to the zany antics of the Coconut Grove Bed Race.

EVENTS

Festivals, parades, and fairs showcase the diverse ethnic backgrounds, interests, and talents of the Miami population. The Goombay Festival brings Caribbean culture to Coconut Grove streets. The Homestead Frontier Days and Rodeo is a legacy of the farming community. The Coconut Grove Arts Festival and the Miami Beach Festival of the Arts are two of the many cultural events. Street fairs such as the Sunstreet Festival and the Orange Blossom Classic Parade and Festival promote neighborhoods. Sports events such as the Lipton International Players Championship and the Doral-Ryder Open are major seasonal events. And some activities are just for fun such as the Coconut Grove Bed Race and the King Mango Strut. But whatever the nature of the event, Miamians love to party. ❖

The International Boat Show and Sailboat Show takes place on land at the Miami Beach Convention Center, but also in the water at the Biscayne Bay Marriott Marina and at the Miami Beach Marina. Boating is big business, but also fun, with shows like the Christmastime Greater Miami Boat Parade, or serious competitions, like the Offshore Professional Tour.

The Nissan Grand Prix borders Biscayne Bay, and therefore attracts a privileged crowd of boat spectators. The racetrack occupies Bicentennial Park and a section of Biscayne Boulevard.

The elegant and powerful of the horse-breeding world enjoy the premier race of the season, the Breeder's Cup, at Gulfstream Park. The race attracts internationally powerful racing figures like the Aga Khan.

Miami is a city of contrasts. Drive a few miles south of downtown, and you enter the Homestead farming community. The annual pageantry elects Miss and Little Miss Frontier Days. It is the home of the Hoe Down and Chili Suppers, Ice Cream Socials, Frontier Days Dances, Beard Growing Contests, and, of course, rodeos. Attracting a large population of Mexican farm workers, Homestead has a Mexican Fiesta with Latin music and marachis.

Opa-Locka airport hosts the Miami Air Show. It would please Glenn Curtiss, Opa-Locka's developer, who was an aviator. Families picnic at the airport among the displayed planes, and for hours watch the Blue Angels, the Golden Knights, or the daredevil, wing-walking Kazians.

Top: Halloween is for costume lovers. *Left:* Christmas is a time for dressing up the boat. *Bottom:* At the Harvest Festival, adults dress in costume to reenact local history. *Opposite, top right:* Artists from the Art Festival visit the local schools, teaching youngsters how to express themselves with paint. *Opposite, bottom left:* At the Coconut Grove Art Festival, Denny Dent, performing painter, dresses himself and his canvasses in paint. *Opposite, top right:* Evening galas with a theme, like *Gone with the Wind* for the Beaux Arts Ball, are opportunities to display one's creative talent. *Opposite, center right:* Tartans are worn at the Key Biscayne Scottish Festival. *Opposite, bottom right:* Period costumes are worn at the Renaissance Festival.

A visitor might conclude that Miamians are artistically spoiled. Besides the exceptional array of visiting international performers, Miami boasts the fifty-year-old Greater Miami Opera, the Florida Philharmonic Orchestra, the New World Symphony, and the Miami City Ballet. The well-established Coconut Grove Playhouse is one of many theaters. Ethnic dance groups like Ballet Flamenco La Rosa perform throughout the year.

The Kiwanis Club of Little Havana presents Carnaval Miami at Bayfront Park, which includes the bike dash and the 8K run. The Junior Orange Bowl Festival offers sport competitions for young people. A strong favorite is the sports event for disabled youth. These athletes practice hard and are determined competitors. The International Tennis Center of Key Biscayne hosts the Lipton International Players Championship. Virginia Key is the home of the Miami Rowing Club. Rowing was brought to Miami by Cubans who had attended east coast universities.

Orange Bowl, Dolphins, Heat, Hurricanes, Doral-Ryder Open, Joe Robbie Stadium, and Lipton are familiar names to Miami sports fans. However, some of the events are not just sport. The Doral-Ryder Open starts the evening before the golf tournament with a concert on the green. The Orange Bowl, now the Federal Express Orange Bowl, begun during the early 1930s to help publicize Miami in the middle of the depression, kicks off with the King Orange Jamboree Parade the night before the football game.

Besides providing entertainment to the public, Miami Seaquarium is a marine research center, and a rescue and rehabilitation institution. Tourists, unfamiliar with manatees, can get acquainted with the herbivorous mammals. Flamingos were first introduced to Miami at Hialeah Park. They now live at Metrozoo and Parrot Jungle. Metrozoo has created habitats that resemble as closely as possible the animals' natural environments.